HAIL! TUDORS

Philip Steele

WAYLAND

WAYLAND

This edition published in 2012 by Wayland

Copyright © 2011 Brown Bear Books Ltd.

Wayland
Hachette Children's Books
338 Euston Road
London NW1 3BH

Wayland Australia
Level 17/207 Kent Street
Sydney, NSW 2000

Brown Bear Books Ltd.
First Floor
9–17 St. Albans Place
London
N1 0NX

Author: Jen Green
Managing editor: Miranda Smith
Designer: Lorna Phillips
Picture researcher: Clare Newman
Design manager: David Poole
Editorial director: Lindsey Lowe
Children's publisher: Anne O'Daly
Consultant: Dr Paul G. Bahn

British Library Cataloguing in Publication Data

Steele, Philip, 1948-
  Tudors. — (Hail!)
  1. Great Britain—History—Tudors, 1485–1603—Juvenile
  literature.
  2. Great Britain—Civilization—16th century—Juvenile
  literature.
  I. Title II. Series
  942'.05-dc23

ISBN–13: 978 0 7502 6746 5

Printed in China

Wayland is a division of Hachette Children's Books, an
Hachette UK company.
www.hachette.co.uk

Websites

The website addresses (URLs) included in this book were valid at the time of going to press. However, because of the nature of the internet, it is possible that some addresses may have changed, or sites may have changed or closed down since publication. While the author and publisher regret any inconvenience this may cause the readers, no responsibility for any such changes can be accepted by either the author or the publisher.

PICTURE ACKNOWLEDGEMENTS
Key: b = bottom, bgr = background, c = centre, is = insert , l = left, mtg = montage, r = right, t = top.

Front Cover: Corbis: Gustavo Tomsich l; Getty Images: Bridgeman Art Library tr, Thinkstock: cr, br.
Interior: Bridgeman Art Library: Historic New England, Boston, Massachusetts, USA 21br; Getty Images: Creativ Studio Heinemann 12tcmontage, Dorling Kindersley 12tc mtg; iStockphoto: Sean Curry 15bcr, Natalia Galkina 21bl, Hulton Archives 15bcl, Rmax 17cl, Duncan Walker 6l, 10cl, 10cr, 11tl, 11bl, 14c, Steven Wynn 26cr; Mary Evans Picture Library: 4; Photolibrary: The National Trust Photo Library 20brt, 21trt; Shutterstock: 24tl, Accent 27bl, Galyna Andrushko 15tlb, Anthro 27br, April Photo 12tc mtg, 17tc, Peter Baxter 6br, Bliznetsov 12br. Katrina Brown 18cl, 18tr, 19tr, 19br, Jirka Bursik 27bc, Rob Byron 29bl, Ilker Canikligi 9c, Jackie Carevy 10tr, 10c, 24c, 25c, 28tl, Cen 12bl, Nicoli Chepe 12tc mtg CLM 5bc, 14tlt, Nicholas Peter Gavin Davies 17cr, Fengya 24tc, Morag Flemming 20bl GJ08 16br. Golden Angel 26clb, Gos Photo Design 12cl, Richard Griffin 25bc, Oli Hnat 13tcb, Stephen Inglis 16bl, Kasia 25tc, Sebastian Kaulitzki 5bcl, 14tlbr, Knorre 3br, 7tc, 17bc, Veniamin Krastov 8tr, Lineartestpilot 27trt, Polina Lobanova 27c, Max Stock Photo 16/17t, 30/31, Vladimir Melnik 12c, Petar Milevasi 18br, Sharon Morris 9clb, 19tl, Christian Musat 12tc mtg, Nanka 15bc, Negib 15trt, O.M. 7bc, Nikolay Okhitin 26bl, Bob Orsillo 27trb, Slavojub Pantelic 24cr, 28br, Kirsty Pargeter 24/25, Mary William Penny 18c, D. Phillips 21trb, Pics Five 18tl, 19ct, Ivan Ponomarev 10tc, Rook 76 26/27 bgr, Atiketta Sangasaeng 5bcr, 14tlbl, Shuttervision 15trb, Hana Sichyngnova 9bc, Natalia Sivenna 16/17, Rose Smith 21cl, Tom Smith 8br, James Steidt 15tlt, Tim Sulov 15cr, 15br, Jonathan M. Thomas 8cl, Olga Tropinina 6tr, Ultimathule 14cr, Natalis Vasina 13tct, Alice 14/15 bgr: Thinkstock: 3tr, 3bc, 5br, 6cr, 7cl, 7tl. 7tr, 8cll, 8clr, 9br, 18bl, 19cb, 19bl, 27tc, 29cr; Topham: 5bl, 11tr, 11br, 16tl, 20tr, 21tl, 26br, 28c, Artmedia/HIP 15br, Roger-Viollet 9clt, 19cr, 29cl, The Granger Collection 25br, 26clt, The Print Collector/HIP 7c, UK City Images 20brb Woodmansterne 13b; Andrew Webb: 10/11 bgr; Wikimedia: 7br.

CONTENTS

THE TUDORS

Let us sound a fanfare for the Tudors, the royal family who changed the history of the British Isles between 1485 and 1603. *HAIL!* sent their journalists to take the pulse of those stormy times. Read their cutting-edge articles about Tudor attitudes to fashion, scandal, fame and power. It is a great story — but were the Tudors marvels or monsters?

LOOKING BACK

The Tudors first ruled England, Wales and Ireland during the final years of the Middle Ages. When their rule ended, the modern world was taking shape. The story of the Tudors starts here....

THE FIRST TUDOR MONARCH

England was torn apart by the Wars of the Roses that began around 1455. Two rival dynasties, York and Lancaster, fought for the throne. In 1485, the exiled Henry Tudor, 2nd Earl of Richmond, landed in Wales. Henry's army defeated and killed Richard III at Bosworth Field, and he was crowned Henry VII, the first ruler of the Tudor dynasty.

Henry VII

TUDOR DYNASTY

Henry VII (1457–1509) m Elizabeth of York

|
Henry VIII (1491–1547)

m

| Catherine of Aragon | Anne Boleyn | Jane Seymour | Anne of Cleves | Kathryn Howard | Katherine Parr |

Mary I (1516–1558) **Elizabeth I** (1533–1603) **Edward VI** (1537–1553)

HAIL! QUIZ WHAT MADE THE TUDORS TICK?

Enter our readers' poll and select your favourite from these five key achievements.

1. THEATRE AND THE ARTS
The Tudor kings and queens were patrons of music, dance, literature and the theatre. The playwright William Shakespeare made his name during the reign of Elizabeth I. His plays would become famous around the world.

2. EXPLORATION
During the Tudor period, the explorer John Cabot sailed from Bristol to reach Newfoundland in Canada; Martin Frobisher explored Canada; Francis Drake sailed around the world; and Sir Walter Raleigh attempted to found a colony in Virginia, North America. The world was opening up to travel and trade.

3. PALACES
Fine palaces were built in England during the Tudor period — Richmond, Hampton Court, Whitehall and Nonesuch. They replaced the old stone castles and were beautifully furnished with tapestries and carved wood. These palaces provided the backdrop to the grand ceremonies and glittering celebrations of the royal court.

4. A GROWING POWER
England began to be rated as a major power in Europe. Henry VIII and later Elizabeth I built a royal navy. England became a serious rival to Spain, whose invading Armada was defeated in 1588.

5. TRADE AND WEALTH
Wool and woollen cloth were the biggest exports at the start of the Tudor period. Lead, tin and coal mines were opened up and flourished. Ships sailed into the port of London from all over Europe — as did treasures looted from Spanish shipping in the New World.

Submit Your Answer

Right Royals! pp.10–11

SEE INSIDE:

Fashion Tips pp. 14–15

Stage people pp. 22–23

REGULAR CONTRIBUTORS:
Henry VIII, Thomas Cromwell, Dr John Dee, Walter Raleigh

HENRY VIII

In his younger days, Henry was hot! At 190 cm (6 ft 3 in), with a 91 cm (36 in) waist, he caused quite a flutter among the ladies of the royal court. Henry was the sporty type, brilliant at indoor tennis and a great gambler.

Kapow!

Another sport for fit young princes in the 1500s? Jousting! In a tournament, you sit on a horse and charge at your opponent, getting points for knocking him off his horse. Henry loves all this medieval stuff. In his suit of armour he was fashionably "dressed to kill"!

WHO ATE ALL THE PIES?

By the time of his death, at 55 years old, Henry VIII was not a pretty sight. He had little eyes in a fat face and his waist had ballooned to 140 cm (55 in). He was covered in boils and it took four strong men to carry him. He probably died of diabetes brought on by his diet and weight.

▲ In his prime, Henry wore the finest clothes and cut a dashing figure.

P. Pauquet

HOW TO LOSE FRIENDS...

Easy, start chopping off their heads! A couple of days after his coronation, Henry had two ministers arrested and executed. Other celebs who got (literally) axed: Sir Thomas More (left), the Bishop of Rochester and Thomas Cromwell (below right). The one thing Henry cannot stand is people who disagree with him. What is the point of being king if you can't get your own way?

Pop Idol!

This king of pop really is a king. Henry VIII is a monarch who just loves to dance. He collects musical instruments, from bagpipes to flutes and virginals, and employs 58 full-time musicians. He enjoys all sorts of sounds, from church and court music to popular love songs. He plays the lute (left) very well, and even writes his own songs.

Greatest Hits
- Hélas Madame
- Pastime with Good Company

SO, WOLSEY...

HAIL! interviewed top political adviser Cardinal Wolsey shortly before he died — on his way to be tried for treason.

"I could see things were getting bad between Henry and myself, so I gave him my palace at Hampton Court, state of the art, all mod cons. And he said, 'Hey, thanks very much, but tough — you're finished anyway.' Well, it seems that he was right on that one. "

French encounter

In 1514, Henry met the French king, François I, for 17 days of sporting combat. The meeting was intended to increase their "bond of friendship". Their camp was called the Field of the Cloth of Gold and it was near Calais in France. Each monarch tried to out do the other — in gold, fancy fashions, flags and pavilions. There were 2,800 tents, fountains running with red wine and 2,200 sheep to be barbecued. It was the party of the century!

François Talks!

King François I of France speaks out

"So Henry and I decided to enter into the spirit of things and have a wrestling match. He was useless! And then he went all moody on everyone because I won. *Sacré bleu,* bad losers, *ces Anglais!* "

LONELY HEARTS

Henry was married six times. He changed the course of history by breaking from the Catholic Church and divorcing his first wife, Catherine of Aragon, to marry Anne Boleyn.

• **Young Spanish** princess, recently widowed, seeks husband. Still has dowry. Used to long engagements.

EXCLUSIVE: Catherine Speaks

Hot Spanish Lover!

"Not only is Henry dumping me for a younger woman but he's saying we were never properly married in the first place. Just because my first husband was his brother! Henry wants a divorce, but the Pope won't let him."

HEADS WILL ROLL

"I have but a little neck"

• **Lady-in-waiting** will wait no longer. Good job (works for queen). Dark hair, brown eyes, six fingers on left hand. Likes fine clothes, jewellery and religious reform.

Henry was desperate to marry Anne Boleyn. The Pope refused to annul Henry's marriage to Catherine, but Henry went ahead anyway. Anne and Henry married in 1533, when she was already pregnant with Elizabeth. The Archbishop of Canterbury declared Henry's first marriage invalid and England broke from the Catholic Church. But Henry tired of Anne. She did not give him a male heir and became unpopular. She was condemned for adultery and was beheaded in 1536.

Lovely But Not Very Well

Jane Seymour caught Henry's eye in 1535. He was certainly keen. They got engaged within 24 hours of Anne Boleyn losing her head and married 3 weeks later. The marriage was happy but short. Their son and heir Edward was born in 1537. But Jane died just two weeks later.

Together forever — Jane was the only wife to be buried with Henry.

• **People say I'm** calm, gentle and demure. But is there more to me than meets the eye? Looking for long-term relationship and possibly more. Keen to provide male heir.

WHAT A MARE!

Anne of Cleves Hits Back!

Henry says he fell in love with my picture but now he calls me the Flanders mare. What an insult! OK, so I'm no oil painting, but look at him! I'm not going to make a fuss. If he wants a divorce, he can have one. I've seen what happened to his other wives. I'll just take the money and the castles and keep quiet.

• **Flemish aristocrat** available for strategic alliance. Easy-going with GSOH. Does not hunt, sing or play a musical instrument. Only speaks German. Fairly attractive; pictures available.

As pretty as a picture?

Rose Without a Thorn

When they married in 1540, Kathryn Howard was 19 while Henry was 49, massive and bloated with a lame leg. Henry was enchanted. He called her his "rose without a thorn" and showered her with gifts. But rumours spread about Kathryn's affairs, and she was executed in 1542.

• **Young, attractive** woman with influential uncle seeks husband. Age no object.

DOMESTIC GODDESS

As someone who has been married twice before, to elderly husbands, Katherine Parr is ideal to become Henry's sixth wife. When Henry began to court Katherine, he had stiff competition in the dashing Sir Thomas Seymour. Henry cunningly arranged for Thomas to be sent as a special ambassador to Belgium and the wedding went ahead. It was a family affair with the king's children all in attendance.

• **Twice widowed,** caring, good with children. Well educated and good at languages (fluent in French, Italian and Latin).

THE HIT LIST

Catherine of Aragon
b.1485, d.1536
Divorced ✖

Anne Boleyn
b.1500?, d.1536
Beheaded 🪓

Jane Seymour
b.1509, d.1537
Died RIP

Anne of Cleves
b.1515, d.1557
Divorced ✖

Kathryn Howard
b.1521, d.1542
Beheaded 🪓

Katherine Parr
b.1512, d.1548
Survived ✔

RIGHT ROYALS!

Those Tudor monarchs really were a mixed bunch — the good, the bad and the ugly! But they knew how to get themselves talked about. Henry and Elizabeth are in all the films and TV shows hundreds of years later ....

" The crown is not my right "

Not a Well Boy

Edward VI took over as king in 1547. His dad was Henry VIII and his mum was wife number 3, Jane Seymour. Edward came to the throne when he was only nine years old. He was educated as a Protestant and the serious business of ruling was left to nobles and relatives. Sadly, young Ed died in 1553, at the age of 15, probably of TB.

A Nine-Day Wonder

When Edward VI was on his death bed, he was persuaded to change his will so that his cousin Lady Jane Grey could become queen. She was another Protestant, a nice and extremely clever young girl, who was being bossed about by grown-ups who wanted power. She was crowned in 1553 but overthrown in just nine days, and some months later had her head cut off.

Did you know?
This was the shortest reign in English history.

She was called Bloody Mary

" I have the heart and stomach of a king "

LOOK AT HER!

Mary had no kids, so the next in line is Princess Elizabeth. Flame-haired Bess loves dancing. She is a real linguist and has her head screwed on (which is just as well in these axe-happy days). She has what it takes and people love her for it. A real celeb, Elizabeth travels all around the country. She rarely misses a painting op (provided it is flattering) and at court every eye is upon her. But she has a fierce temper, just like her dad!

CONTRARY MARY

The second coronation in 1553 was for Mary I, daughter of Henry and wife number 1, Catherine of Aragon. Mary really was not a merry monarch. She did not like Anne Boleyn's daughter Elizabeth being around. Mary was Catholic and could not stand Protestants. She had nearly 300 of them burnt alive during her reign, which lasted five years until her death in 1558.
PS: Mary did like the Catholic king, Philip II of Spain — in fact she married him!

So how did a King of Spain make out as King of England? *HAIL!* travelled to the land of oranges and castles to ask the man himself.

" OK, I admire the lady a lot. She's a good Catholic, but a little bit weird, if you know what I mean? And she's not getting any younger. And the weather there's not so sunny. *Dios mio, los Ingleses* are a little bit miserable, are they not? "

A Royal Wedding? Will she, won't she?

Elizabeth has certainly liked to keep her admirers guessing! But is that just a smart political move? And now she says she will not marry anyone at all! But there are rumours that she and Robert Dudley are more than just good friends!

What's in your FRIDGE?

Tudors liked meat, and lots of it. It was roasted, boiled and put into pies. Food could not be frozen so it was preserved or eaten fresh.

Did you know?

Sugar is a luxury and only for the rich. Most people use honey as a sweetener.

Meat
Hares, pigs, deer, calves and wild boar are popular. All parts of the animal are eaten.

Birds
Swans, pheasants, herons, bitterns, partridges, quails, pigeons, larks, chickens and sparrows are all on the menu.

Fish and seafood
Fish is eaten on Fridays and during Lent. Choose from eels, pike, salmon, whiting, haddock, bass, carp, crabs or lobster.

Spices
Meat is salted or pickled to last longer. Spices such as pepper, nutmeg and ginger are useful to disguise the salt and the taste of rotten meat.

Vegetables
Eaten in small amounts and only when in season.

Soup, soup and more soup

Food for the poor is pottage (soup made of herbs) and bread.

BREAD BASKET

Bread is served at every meal. Poor people eat carter's bread. Made from rye and wheat, it is black or dark brown in colour. Rich people eat a fine, white bread called manchet. In between is ravelled bread, made from wholewheat flour with the bran left in.

Our nutritionist says:

• This is a typical Tudor diet, high in protein, fats and sugars. Bad teeth and skin disease are common.
• Don't drink the water! Rich people drink wine, and everyone drinks ale.
• Dairy foods, fresh fruit and root vegetables are eaten by the poor.

HOW TO THROW A DINNER PARTY

Feasts and banquets were lavish affairs with lots of dishes, the finest ingredients and unusual recipes.

Menu

First Course
Brawn (boar meat)
Roast tongue
Leg of pork
Roast beef
Roast venison
Meat pie
Vegetables in season

Second Course
Roast lamb,
Rabbit, Bread

Dessert
Tarts and custard

Sheep's Feet

To make the best sheep's feet Take sheep's feet, slit the bone and pick them very clean. Place in frying pan, with a ladleful of strong broth and butter.

To impress guests, serve a cockatrice (the front of a rooster sewn to the back of a pig) or roasted peacock served in its own skin.

DOs AND DON'Ts

✔ Do wash your hands where everyone can see them. You'll be taking food from shared plates so people will want to see that your hands are clean.

✖ Don't put your fingers in your ears while you're eating, and don't blow your nose on your napkin.

✔ Do throw the bones on the floor when you've picked aff the meat.

✖ Don't forget to bring your own knife and spoon.

✖ Don't drink the water! It will only make you sick. Drink ale, beer or wine.

STATE-OF-THE-ART KITCHEN

Hurry! Sale ends soon!

Modern kitchens

• Henry VIII's kitchens at Hampton Court are state-of-the-art. They have 50 rooms and measure an amazing 3,345 square metres (36,000 sq. ft).

• Diners there drink 600 barrels of alcohol a year.

• Roast beef takes nine hours to cook. The spit has to be kept turning all the time the meat is roasting.

• Strict laws say who can sit where — and how much food they can be served.

FASHION, FOLLIES & FARTHINGALES

The royal court was the Tudor catwalk. The ladies dressed to impress, and Henry was often very impressed indeed. It was different with Elizabeth. She liked to be the centre of attention and nobody was allowed to outshine her.

WHAT'S REALLY IN FOR A GIRLS' NIGHT OUT?

Ruffles
Lacy ruffs around the neck, to frame the face!

Pearls
Pearls — in your ears, on your bodice, on your headdress or those elegant gloves....

Big Skirt
Big skirts, stiff and fitted around hoops called farthingales. These are made of willow or whalebone.

Fabric
Make the most of gorgeous fabrics with a "slash" that reveals the satins and silks.

A TIGHT FIT

Do you want really tight sleeves — the height of fashion? Make them detachable so that they are pinned on or even sewn on each time you wear that dress. Too much hard work? Your maidservants can unpick them for you afterwards.

Washing did you say?

Most people in Tudor times are quite content to wash once every three months, or even less often. After all, who needs to wash when there is perfectly good musk and civet perfume to be purchased down at Cheapside? Queen Elizabeth, on the other hand, likes a hot bath, or so the story goes.

HOT ROCKS

Tudor courtiers, both men and women, wear heaps of fabulously expensive jewellery. Fashions from continental Europe are much in vogue — gleaming pearls, rich gold, cool silver, fiery rubies or green emeralds from the New World. Elaborate pendants hang from gold chains or silk ribbons. Brooches, or pins, are worn on hats or clothes.

Fancy Threads

Tudor men are as much fashion victims as the women, with their ruffs, doublets and hose, richly embroidered cloth and fancy earrings. Of course, that is only if you are a courtier. You will wear a less decorative suit if you are a merchant or a businessman. And smelly old rags if you are a beggar — but hey ho, that's life.

Don't Let On!

Sneak a look inside Queen Elizabeth's private chambers! She has 1,000 dresses! And over 80 wigs and hairpieces!

Make-up tips

- Perfumes, creams and oils are just so necessary for your skin. Some are made from beeswax.

- Use cinnabar, madder or cochineal for lips and cheeks, henna for nails and hair.

- White make-up for a pale face or to cover smallpox scars? Wrinkles or pimples to hide? Lay it on thick! Watch out — this make-up is made from poisonous lead.

THOMAS CROMWELL

 ESTATE AGENTS

Selling Out

Henry VIII wanted to divorce Catherine of Aragon in order to marry Anne Boleyn, who he thought would give him a male heir. He fell out with the Pope over this and, in 1534, declared himself head of the Church of England. He decided to shut down about 850 monasteries, convents and religious shrines. He was hard up and the monks had fabulous treasures and huge estates. Henry's old friend Thomas Cromwell filled the royal coffers with the proceeds.

ABBEYS AT SLASHED PRICES!

HURRY WHILE STOCKS LAST!!

GLASTONBURY ABBEY, SOMERSET
One of the most famous monasteries in the land, founded in the 600s. Renowned in myth and legend. Abbot recently executed for not cooperating.

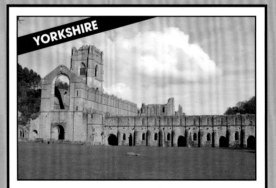

FOUNTAINS ABBEY, YORKSHIRE
New on the market, handed over by an abbot in return for an annual pension. Just perfect for property development. A real bargain.

AMAZING DEALS TO BE HAD — ESPECIALLY IF YOU ARE A PAL OF HENRY VIII OR THOMAS CROMWELL

By appointment to
HIS ROYAL HIGHNESS HENRY VIII

Clearance sale of extensive properties and assets formerly in the possession of the Roman Catholic Church

HOW THE SCAM WORKS

1 Send in the commissioners, who accuse the monks of wrong-doing.
2 Seize all money, treasure, books and precious furnishings.
3 Sell off the land to supporters of the king and friends of Thomas Cromwell, in return for loyalty.
4 Knock down buildings and sell materials to local people, and rent out parcels of land.
5 Spend the proceeds on new wars!

HAIL! met up with one of the monks packing his bags. How did he feel?

Between you and me, the abbot did drink a bit too much and some of the monks were up to no good. But that Thomas Cromwell pretends to be Mr. Morality, when the only thing that makes him tick is power. Without any monks and nuns, who will look after the poor and sick?

Heads off

OK, Thomas Cromwell was not really an estate agent. But he was the wheeler-dealer who got this scam going. He made lots of money and was created Earl of Essex. But he got on the wrong side of Henry VIII over the disastrous marriage deal with Anne of Cleves and had his head cut off (then boiled and stuck on a spike). That was in July 1540.

NORTH IN REVOLT

YORK, 1536

They are calling it "the Pilgrimage of Grace". Across northern England, Catholics have had enough of the king's tyrannical behaviour. In York, 9,000 protesters (the king's men claim fewer) have all but taken over the city. Hopes are high that Henry will make his peace with the rebels.

York Minster

LONDON, 1537

Despite the deal he made with the rebels, Henry has decided to impose martial law on the north and execute 216 rebels anyway, including nobles, abbots and monks. Now there's a surprise!

LAW & ORDER

The law courts of the Tudors were actually pretty fair. But the sentences could be severe. In Elizabeth's reign, new laws made things a bit easier for the poor, and that helped cut crime. But on the streets of London there were still spies, secret agents, muggers and murderers....

VAGABOND!

Why do I wander from town to town? Because I used to graze my cows on the common, but they fenced it all off, so I had no work, so I couldn't pay rent. I used to go up to the monastery where they'd give me a bit of work, or some bread and salted herring. Then they shut down the monastery. Now I get whipped from town to town. The king has got a lot to answer for!

I WORK FOR FOOD!

HAIL! QUIZ OF THE WEEK

What kind of criminal are you?

- **Homeless vagrant**
  Punishment: whipped out of town.

- **Beggar, cheat, or conman**
  Punishment: locked in the stocks or pillory, where people chuck rubbish at you.

- **Thief, murderer or contract killer**
  Punishment: hanged on the public gallows.

- **Heretic** (practicing the wrong religious beliefs)
  Punishment: burned alive at the stake.

- **Traitor or conspirator**
  Punishment: hanged, drawn and quartered. *

*The convicted traitor is hanged until not quite dead. His guts are cut out and burned. The body is then beheaded and chopped into four parts. These are put on public display in different parts of the city.

gallows

stocks

Submit Your Answer

KNOW THE CANT!

Some of the language on the streets of London is called "cant", a secret lingo known only to the criminal underworld. Here are some of the words they use:

Angler A thief who uses a hooked pole to steal items through open windows.

Bawdy-basket A door-to-door seller who befriends servants in order to steal.

Coney-catcher A conman who swindles you out of your money.

Counterfeit crank A beggar who pretends to be an invalid.

Cutpurse A mugger, a robber.

Dell Homeless woman or runaway maidservant, living off crime.

Kinchin mort A baby or young girl used for begging and stealing.

Prigger A horse thief.

Ruffler A fancy-dressing villain or bully, often an old soldier.

Keeping watch

HAIL! comes across a guardian of the peace on his nightly round.

"TWELVE OF THE CLOCK, LOOK WELL TO YOUR LOCKS!"

Q *"Excuse me, officer, why are you yelling and ringing your bell at midnight?"*

A "To let evildoers know that the forces of law and order are on patrol."

Q *"What's your job, exactly?"*

A "Parish constable, member of the Watch for the last five years. I don't catch many villains, but my dog puts the fear of the Lord in 'em!"

SPYMASTER "W"

Sir Francis Walsingham is a grey, shadowy figure, a genius at sniffing out treason and plots against Queen Elizabeth. He has secret agents everywhere, in England and across Europe. Watch out, you traitors!

GRISLY STABBING IN DEPTFORD

Famous playwright Kit Marlowe killed in drunken brawl!

LONDON, 30 May 1593

London was awash with rumours today after the death of top drama writer Kit Marlowe in a tavern. His murderers were said to be members of an underworld gang. Do they have links with the Secret Service? Was Marlowe really an agent himself? Was he really a dangerous atheist? Was he just drunk? And were his plays any good? We demand to know whether there has been a cover-up!

WELCOME TO MY
BEAUTIFUL HOME!

We go inside a choice selection of Tudor homes to admire the decor, furnishings and location. How would you give them a makeover?

All mod cons

No more drafty old castles for the royals. This is the age of luxury palaces, with big fireplaces and tall chimneys. The ultimate new residence has to be Nonesuch Palace, near Epsom in Surrey (right). They say it cost Henry VIII a veritable fortune, so only suitable for the Tudor billionaire!

LOCATION LOCATION

Hardwick Hall, Derbyshire
Hilltop site. Built for the Countess of Shrewsbury in the 1590s. Huge windows to let in the light and show how much money she spent on glass.

Newlands Farm, Stratford-upon-Avon
Later known as Anne Hathaway's Cottage, this was the childhood home of William Shakespeare's wife. That rural look includes a thatched roof and half timbering, and there is a lovely cottage garden.

Plas Mawr, Conwy, Wales
This fine townhouse was built in 1577–85 for a wealthy Welsh gent called Robert Wynn. Urban setting with brewhouse, kitchens and pantry.

Interior Design

Oak panelling? Flemish tapestry? Decorated ceilings? Show just how stylish you can be.

• A quiet word of advice: a few Tudor rose logos (below right) help to show whose side you are on.

• That polished oak look is a classic, and will really last. Show off the finest carving on chests and cupboards — and the legs of thrones (above right).

• Four-poster beds (left) keep out the drafts and are very cosy and comfy. But the finishing touch is the chic fabric chosen for the bedspread!

Beware those smells!

If you are a royal, then it is best to move from one palace to another at the end of each season. The toilets do get rather smelly, and the palaces can be given a good clean while you are away.

There are no proper sewers or drains. If you own a townhouse, then you'll be well aware of the odour that hits you on the rat-infested streets every day. And foul smells bring diseases with them.

The garden scene

 In vogue for Tudor garden designs are intricate "knot" patterns of low hedges (above) and gravel paths. You could add a maze as a puzzle for your guests, or a fountain to tinkle away on a summer's day.

 Border the paths with fragrant shrubs such as rosemary and lavender. These can be strewn on the floors of the house to keep it smelling sweet.

✿ Scented flowers can make sweet bouquets or nosegays to keep away the plague. And all sorts of medicinal plants, such as rhubarb, can sort out a bad tummy or headache.

BEHIND THE SCENES

***HAIL!*'s reporters go behind the scenes at a big country house...**

Q *So you are a maidservant here? You must be proud to work in such a lovely house.*

A I don't know about that, I'm certainly exhausted! All those stairs! All that water to carry from the well in the yard!

Q *Do they treat you well?*

A Lady P. is alright, but that daughter's stuck-up!

Q *What are you up to now?*

A Carrying a warming pan up to my lady's bedroom. Must dash.

Warming pan

What's on in TUDOR TOWN?

★★★★☆

Cockfight

Traditional Shrove Tuesday entertainment. Two one-year-old cockerels fighting — see the feathers fly and place your bets!

Globe Theatre, London

Another chance to catch the popular play *Romeo and Juliet* by William Shakespeare. A real heartbreaker!

Grand Ball At The Royal Court

Fashion heaven! Strictly for courtiers, though, or foreign ambassadors. You might just catch glimpses of their carriages as you wait in the wind and the rain. And inside the palace (left), there is such dancing and merriment!

London Bear-Garden And Bull Ring Theatre

See the mastiffs go in and bait the bulls and bears! Watch as big sums of money are won or lost! Even Queen Elizabeth has been known to drop by to watch the blood flow.

May Day Revels

Anywhere in the kingdom on 1 May you will find houses decked in greenery, the May Queen and Jack O'Green, drums and dancing. See St. George fight the Dragon! Watch amazing amounts of ale flow!

Midsummer Bonfires

See in Midsummer's Eve with bells and bonfires. But keep clear of any religious types who might object!

★ ★ ★ ★ ☆

HAIL!'s Party People team is here to help you find out what is going on. Are you visiting London or are you travelling around the country? Wherever you go, there are always a lot of laughs to be had. And cultural feasts can be found in the most unlikely places!

All the world's a stage

There is a new play on the London stage that is sure to become a smash hit. The writer is Master Will Shakespeare, who has taken the capital by storm in recent years. *The Tragedy of Hamlet, Prince of Denmark* has the lot: a murder, a ghost, madness, love and a play within the play. At the end, the corpses are piled high! Even the groundlings, the mob in the open yard at the front of the stage, fell silent. Actor Richard Burbage masters his leading role.

RATING ★ ★ ★ ☆

QUEEN LAUGHS HERSELF TO BITS!

Queen Elizabeth I admitted last night that she is the number 1 fan of Shoreditch-based comic Richard Tarlton, everyone's favourite stand-up (or fall-down)! It is a well-known fact that all players are rogues, but few players are like our Richard. He has made his name by taking on hecklers and winning. He is a brilliant clown who makes up witty songs on the spot.

RATING
★ ★ ★ ☆

STOP PRESS

LONDON, 12 June 1599

This evening sees the opening night at the Globe Theatre (left), built by the Lord Chamberlain's Men, the actors company who are shareholders in this enterprise. Richard Burbage and his brother Cuthbert own 25 percent each, while William Shakespeare (the playwright of the company) and three others own 12.5 percent each. They have built the theatre on some marshy gardens in Southwark, south London.

YOUR LETTERS

**Got a problem? Share it with our readers.
Our WISE WOMAN offers the best advice....**

*Dear Wise Woman,
I just don't seem to be able to hold
down a relationship. I am now
on my sixth wife. I'm a good catch,
you'd have thought I would have
found Mistress Right by now.*

Henry R, Hampton Court

Dear Henry R,
Hasn't it ever occurred to you that it's you
who might be Master Wrong? Lose some
weight, tidy yourself up! Perhaps you're the
sort of person who chops off people's heads.
Don't if you want a friend as well as a wife!

*Dear Wise Woman,
I rule a kingdom, but I only
have the body of a weak and
feeble woman. My Spanish
brother-in-law is sending a
war fleet or Armada to invade
my country. What can I do?*

Elizabeth R, Greenwich

*Dear Wise Woman,
My son, William really is a lazy so-and-so.
His first Latin lesson at the grammar school
doesn't start until the very reasonable hour
of seven in the morning, but can I get him
out of bed? He creeps like a snail to school,
most unwillingly.*

Stratford-upon-Avon

Dear Mistress S,
I blame the teachers. Your son is obviously not
being beaten enough with those birch twigs!
If you spare the rod, you will spoil the child.

Dear Elizabeth R,
Your brother-in-law sounds like a
real bully. Why don't you call all
your soldiers and sailors together
and tell them that you have the
heart and stomach of a king.
I am sure they'll all cheer and
send him and his so-called
Armada packing. Atta girl!

Dear Wise Woman,

I'm Queen of Scots, and when I got chucked out of Scotland, I thought I'd go and stay with my cousin Bess, who's Queen of England. OK, she's a Protestant and I'm a Catholic, but I did expect some hospitality, since we're family. I got hospitality alright — at Her Majesty's pleasure. Imprisoned for 19 years! Life is SO unfair!

Mary Stuart, Fotheringhay Castle

WISE WOMAN WRITES:

Dear Mary, Queen of Scots,
You have every right to be angry. What are families like these days? Now don't lose your head, it might never happen. On the other hand, it might, so you'd better start saying your prayers.

Sadly, since this letter appeared in our columns, Mary, Queen of Scots has been executed. We extend our sympathy to her family and friends — and her poor little dog.

Is it Really All in the Stars?

The queen's personal astrologer, Dr. John Dee, looks into his crystal ball for *HAIL!*

I welcome this chance to have a chat with the readers of *HAIL!* As you know I am a mathematician and scientist with a long beard, so I do live in the real world. I can confirm that the stars and planets have an influence on our daily lives. It is as obvious as the fact that metals of no value can be turned into solid gold. We can indeed predict the future, and speak with angels and the spirits of the dead.

TRAVEL SUPPLEMENT

The Tudor era was the age of exploration, particularly by sea. New worlds awaited adventurous travellers. We look at some of those brave souls who set sail for far-flung, and often dangerous, lands.

GO FOR GOLD!

Sir Martin Frobisher fancied a trip to China, but instead went to Canada — three times! He brought back tons of "gold", but it was actually worthless iron pyrites — "fool's gold".

Tip: Travellers need to do their homework properly.

Beware unseen dangers

Sir Francis Drake sailed round the entire world. He got rich, he saw amazing sights and managed to dodge both the cannonballs and the cannibals. But he did get a terrible stomach bug on a trip to Panama, and sadly it finished him off!

Tip: Don't drink the local water.

WIN YOUR OWN GLOBE

Just like the queen's. But there are still a few bits that are blank, as there are so many places to explore.

Eldorado no-show

Walter Raleigh was the guy who, in 1584, began a colony at Virginia, in North America, naming it after "the Virgin Queen," Elizabeth I. He went to South America and heard these rumours about a fabulous place called Eldorado. He wrote all about it, and later, James I sent Walter off to find it. But it did not exist! Heads rolled, alas.

Tip: Don't believe all the travel books!

Wonders of the world

The great thing about Tudor seafarers whizzing around the world is that they can tell us about the lands they have seen and whether all those old medieval travellers' tales were really true or not.

HAIL! can now absolutely confirm that unicorns, dragons and mermaids exist — the evidence comes from sailors who have seen them! We just cannot wait to see these amazing sights with our own eyes.

PIRATE FORECAST

Do you fancy a sunny Mediterranean cruise, or a fishing trip closer to home? Never set off on holiday without checking our pirate forecast, or you may end up as a galley slave.

- **North African Coast** — Fierce activity by Barbary corsairs in search of Christian slaves and treasure.

- **West Coast of Ireland** — Grainne ni Mhaille (we call her Grace O'Malley) has been running a pirate fleet out of Clew Bay, but the rumour is she's ready to do a peace deal with Queen Elizabeth herself.

- **North Sea** — Things are more peaceful since Klein Hänslein and 33 other pirates were beheaded in Hamburg in 1573.

Psst! Do readers remember Thomas Stukeley, accused of piracy in 1558? The one who later rebelled against Queen Elizabeth? Well, people say his father might have been Henry VIII himself! A real Tudor pirate....

HAIL!'S TRIBUTE TO THE PASSING OF AN AGE

118 GLORIOUS YEARS

Sad to say, the age of the Tudors has come to an end. In this issue we commemorate the reign of Queen Elizabeth I and mark the end of the Tudor dynasty.

24 March, 1603
For some months the Queen has been in poor health and really not looking herself at all. We must now report that in the early hours of this morning, Elizabeth I passed away peacefully at Richmond Palace at the age of 69.

What a send-off!

You should have seen the funeral of Elizabeth I. The horses were draped in black velvet, the banners with the royal coats-of-arms held high, and every noble in the land was in the procession to Westminster Abbey (below). Crowds packed the streets and rooftops to see the passing of an era.

Did you know?

On the top of the coffin was a full-sized model of the queen, made from wax. It was dressed in the queen's richest robes. A crown was placed on the head and a sceptre in her hand.

WHO WILL INHERIT?

That is the question that has been on everyone's lips for months. Elizabeth had no husband — despite all her suitors — so no children to inherit the throne. We all fear for our future.

UNDER NEW MANAGEMENT

The Stuarts were the royal family of Scotland. They were related by marriage to the Tudors and became the next rulers of England and Wales. A horseman galloped from London to Scotland in just three days to carry the news to the future James I.

Meet the Stuarts

King James VI of Scotland will be known as James I south of the border, becoming king of both countries. This is an amazing turn of events, because it was his mother, Mary, Queen of Scots, who was executed by Queen Elizabeth back in 1587.

Did you know?

King James is a bit of a campaigner. He has a thing about witches and also about that newfangled weed, tobacco. He does not approve of either!

LOOKING BACK

How did people remember the Tudor age? At the time, people did not like the Tudors much, and even Elizabeth was not popular in old age.

But the Stuarts were so incredibly stuck-up and bossy that in the end people decided to cut off a king's head! In 1649, they executed Charles I. By then, people were recalling Tudor times as the "good old days of jollity, roast beef and Good Queen Bess". That's nostalgia for you!

Charles I

HAIL! has found some old fogies who still remember the Tudors

"I tell you what, it was more peaceful in England and Wales in those days. There were wars in other places of course, but I never had to fight."

"Tudors? Stuarts? They're all the same if you ask me. We poor folk still have to plough the fields, and the roof of our cottage still leaks."

"Oh my grandfather did frightfully well back in the days of Henry VIII. We made our fortune, and we are still rich today."

GLOSSARY

civet A very strong scent given out by a mammal called the African civet, used in the making of perfumes.

cochineal A natural red dye exported to Europe from the New World as early as the 1500s. It is made from insects.

Flemish Describes someone coming from Flanders, a lowland region now occupied by parts of France, Belgium and the Netherlands. Also the language spoken there, a form of Dutch.

henna A natural reddish brown dye obtained from a flowering plant grown in Africa and Asia.

madder A natural reddish pink dye obtained from the root of the common madder plant.

martial law Military rule by a state over its citizens in times of emergency.

mastiff The English mastiff, a large, heavy breed of dog used for guard duty as well as bull-baiting and bear-baiting.

Midsummer's Eve A pre-Christian festival held on 23 June, marked by bonfires and feasts. In Tudor times the merriment continued, although it was by then known as St John's Eve.

pillory A form of public punishment, made up of a wooden frame that locked around the head and hands of the prisoner. People threw things such as rubbish at the prisoner.

plague A deadly infection of the lungs, the blood or the lymph nodes. Spread by rats, the plague was common in medieval, Tudor and the later Stuart times.

Shrove Tuesday The last day before the Christian fasting period known as Lent. Also known as Mardi Gras.

stocks A form of public punishment, made up of a wooden frame that locked around the feet of the prisoner. People would be kept in the stocks for a few hours.

tapestry A woven wall hanging, featuring designs or pictures.

TB Tuberculosis, a deadly infection that normally attacks the lungs.

tyrannical Behaving like a tyrant or a despot, being cruel or harsh.

virginals A musical instrument with a keyboard, rather like a harpsichord.

1485 Battle of Bosworth Field; Henry VII becomes the first Tudor king

1520 Field of the Cloth of Gold meeting in France between Henry VIII and François I

1533 Henry VIII marries Anne Boleyn

1547 Edward VI becomes king of England

1450

1525

1545

1509 Henry VIII becomes king and marries his first wife, Catherine of Aragon

1531 Henry VIII becomes head of the Church of England and Wales

1535 Start of the Dissolution (closing down) of the Monasteries

ON THE WEB

www.bbc.co.uk/history/british/tudors/ Excellent site covering everything from the *Mary Rose*, Henry VIII's flagship, to daily life and Tudor spies.

www.nationalarchives.gov.uk/education/lesson39.htm Original documents about the Spanish Armada, and searching questions.

www.spartacus.schoolnet.co.uk/Tudors.htm Comprehensive site including biographies, events, the theatre, poverty and religion.

www.historylearningsite.co.uk/tudor_england.htm Many articles on the major events and big personalities that dominated Tudor history.

www.tudorhistory.org/ Family trees, photos, timelines and lists.

www.elizabethan-era.org.uk/ Food, clothes, sports, exploration, music and other Tudor topics.

www.globe-theatre.org.uk/ History of the famous London stage, its actors, audiences and its most famous playwright William Shakespeare.

www.localhistories.org/tudor.html Education, medicine, homes and other aspects of Tudor social history.

BOOKS

A Tudor Journey by Philip Steele (Wayland, 2003)

Britain Through the Ages: Tudors by Felicity Hebditch (Evans Brothers, 2003)

People in the Past: Tudor Rich and Poor by Haydn Middleton (Heinemann Library, 2004)

Eyewitness: Tudor by Simon Adams (Dorling Kindersley, 2008)

Henry VIII: Royal Beheader by Sean Stewart Price (Franklin Watts, 2009)

The Gruesome Truth About the Tudors by Jillian Powell (Wayland, 2010)

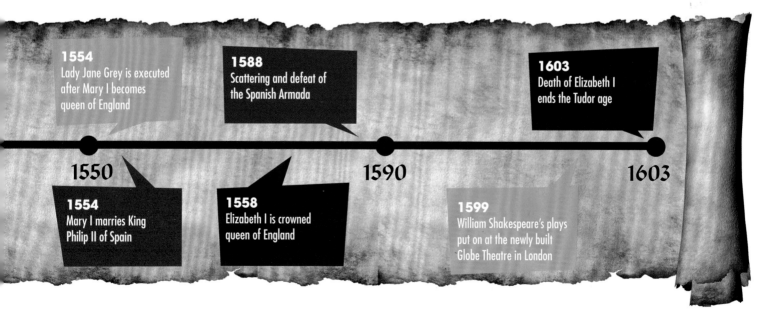

1554 Lady Jane Grey is executed after Mary I becomes queen of England

1588 Scattering and defeat of the Spanish Armada

1603 Death of Elizabeth I ends the Tudor age

1550

1590

1603

1554 Mary I marries King Philip II of Spain

1558 Elizabeth I is crowned queen of England

1599 William Shakespeare's plays put on at the newly built Globe Theatre in London

INDEX